WIZOO Quick Start

Craig Anderton

Audio Mastering

(:wizoo:)

Imprint

Author   Craig Anderton
Publisher   Peter Gorges

Cover art   design box, Ravensburg, Germany
Editor   Reinhard Schmitz
Interior design and layout   Uwe Senkler

Order No.   WZ 00726
International Standard Book Number   0-8256-1937-8

Exclusive Distributors:
Music Sales Corporation
257 Park Avenue South, New York, NY 10010 USA

Music Sales Limited
8/9 Frith Street, London W1D 3JB England

Music Sales Pty. Limited
120 Rothschild Street, Rosebery, Sydney, NSW 2018, Australia

Printed in the United States of America
by Vicks Lithograph and Printing Corporation

Welcome

For many years, mastering was an esoteric art that required very expensive tools. Thanks to computers, mastering tools are now widely available at a reasonable price, making it possible to learn mastering on a setup that most musicians can afford.

Like all Wizoo Quick Starts, this book is designed to help you get a handle on this topic as quickly as possible. It's written in concise, easy-to-understand language, and includes a CD-ROM packed with WAV file examples.

However, please note that mastering is an art that relies on experience and feel as well as technique. This book can only describe how the tools work; how you apply them is what makes one mastering engineer different from another. Mastering is an exacting blend of art and science, but be persistent. Learning any musical instrument takes time—a mastering studio is very much like an instrument.

Here's hoping you enjoy reading, listening, and finding your ultimate sound. I wish you lots of success as you learn your way. But above all, have fun!

Peter Gorges, Publisher

Table of Contents

1 What Is Mastering?   7

About Frequency Response and Hearing   7
Mastering Tasks   9

2 Mastering Tools   11

Plug-in Formats   12
Inserting Plug-ins   14

3 Parametric EQ   16

Parametric EQ Basics   16
Parametric Controls   17
Variations   17
Applying Parametric EQ   21

4 Curve Analysis/Matching   24

Spectrum Analyzers   24
Spectrum Display Meets EQ   25

5 About Dynamics   28

About Headroom   29
About Normalization   29
Why Compression Makes Songs Louder   30
Use Your Judgement   31

6 Compression   32

Compressor Parameters   32
Miscellaneous Parameters   34
How to Adjust Compression   34

7 Multiband Compression   36

8 Level Maximizers   38

Level Maximizer Basics   38
Using Level Maximizers   39

9 Dithering   40

10 Specialized Tools   41

Vintage Device Emulators   41
Bass Enhancers   42
Stereo Image Enhancers   42
Harmonic Enhancers   43
Reverb   43

11 Troubleshooting   44

12 FAQ   45

13 CD-ROM Files   47

14 Internet Links   48

What Is Mastering? 1

Mastering is the stage between mixing and the pressing plant where you assemble your tunes in the proper order and process them if necessary. As the final link in the CD production chain, mastering can make or break a project—which is why people pay big bucks to a veteran mastering engineer for an objective viewpoint. Unless you have much experience, hiring someone who really knows how to master could be the best move for your music.

On the other hand, one way to get that experience is to try it yourself. If nothing else, you'll appreciate the role of mastering better, and communicate more effectively should you use professional mastering services.

> Mastering is not intended to salvage a recording, but enhance an already superb mix. If there's a problem with the mix, remix the tune—don't count on mastering to solve the problem.

About Frequency Response and Hearing

One goal of mastering is to produce a balanced, even sound. A well-mastered recording has a full, satisfying bass without "muddiness," a well-defined midrange, and sparkly (not screechy) highs.

To achieve this, we need to understand frequency response.

Hz measures the number of cycles per second in a wave. 1kHz = 1000Hz.

Frequency response defines how a system records or reproduces the spectrum of audible frequencies which stretches from 20Hz to 20,000Hz. This is usually shown on a graph. The Y-axis (vertical) shows level, and the X-axis (horizontal) indicates frequency.

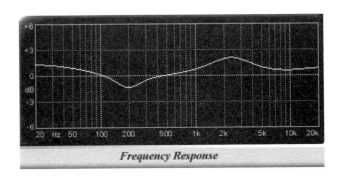

Frequency Response

The audible range is further divided into bands. These are not precisely defined, but here's a rough guide.

❖ Bass: Lowest frequencies, typically below 200Hz

❖ Lower midrange: 200 to 800Hz

❖ Midrange: 800Hz to 2.5kHz

❖ Upper midrange: 2.5kHz to 8kHz

❖ Treble: 8kHz and higher

While these guidelines are approximate, they are still useful as references. Examples: Bass guitar and kick drum occupy the bass range. Vocals are in the midrange and lower midrange. Percussion instruments like tambourine have lots of energy in the treble region.

A system with a flat frequency response means that no range of frequencies is accented or diminished.

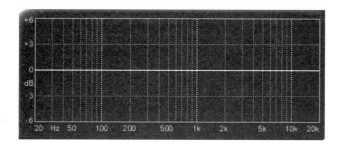

Although electronic devices like hi-fi amplifiers often have a flat frequency response, no mechanical device does. A speaker's response falls off at high and low frequencies. Guitar pickup response falls off at high frequencies which is why guitar amps often boost the upper midrange.

The ear's response is not flat. As a person ages, high frequency response diminishes. But even for those with healthy ears, high and low frequency response drops off at soft volumes. At high levels, the high and low frequencies sound more prominent.

Realistically, you can't accommodate all these variables. When mastering, strive for a good average response that sounds good over as many systems as possible.

Because the ear's frequency response changes depending on level, if you master at too low a level, you might boost the bass and treble too much. Master at a comfortable listening level—not too loud or soft. Then check at both high and low levels to find a good average setting.

Mastering Tasks

The mastering process addresses several issues:

❖ *Equalization*. This balances out the frequency response. Equalization can even affect the mix by emphasizing the frequency range of particular instruments.

Equalization is a fancy word for "tone control." It can reduce the bass for muddy recordings, increase treble for dull recordings, and so on.

Dynamic range is the difference between a tune's loudest and softest parts. Most pop music has a limited dynamic range, whereas classical music has a wide dynamic range.

❖ Song-to-song levels. You don't want huge volume variations among songs.

❖ Fade ins, fade outs, and crossfades. Add these when assembling the tunes.

❖ Compression/limiting. This can help even out the *dynamic range*, both within a song and within the context of the overall CD.

❖ Occasional effects. Adding a bit of reverb can help smooth over an abrupt cut or tight splice.

❖ Cleanup. This is your last chance to remove any remaining noise, hum, pops, clicks, crackles, etc.

Mastering Tools

2

The least expensive way to master your music is with a Windows or Mac computer. You will also need the following tools.

❖ A high-quality monitoring system and good acoustic environment. You can't master music accurately if you don't hear it accurately. For most situations, near-field monitoring speakers are best. Place them in an equilateral triangle with your head forming one point, and the speakers about 2 to 3 feet away from your ears, at ear level. Listening to the speakers directly minimizes the effects of room acoustics.

❖ Digital audio editing program. Typical examples for Windows are Sonic Foundry's Sound Forge, Steinberg's WaveLab, Magix Samplitude Master, and Syntrillium's Cool Edit; for Mac, there's BIAS Peak, Prosoniq sonicWORX, and TC Works' Spark. These programs display digital audio as waveforms where you can cut, paste, and otherwise manipulate audio files.

Many shareware audio editors are available; do a search on the web to find these. Sometimes, "light" versions of costly programs come bundled with sound cards.

❖ High-capacity hard disk. A CD-length project (about 60 minutes) chews up over 600MB of sound. You'll probably need room for a backup file too, so you'll want to dedicate several Gigabytes to mastering projects.

"Plug-ins" get their name because hardware signal processors "plug in" to a mixer or patchbay. The software equivalent plugs into a host program, like a digital audio editor.

❖ Software signal processors. Although digital audio editing programs often include common signal processors, mastering engineers sometimes need specialized processors. So, editing programs usually offer a way to "plug in" accessory programs from other manufacturers. These programs, called "plug-ins," provide a variety of functions, including some dedicated specifically to mastering.

Check that your program supports the CD burner you want to use. The software manufacturer's web site usually lists supported drives.

❖ CD burner. After creating your master, you'll want to burn a CD copy so you can test it under a variety of listening conditions. Your computer or digital audio editor may have dedicated CD-burning software, or you may need to purchase a separate package.

Plug-in Formats

Real-time plug-ins are becoming the dominant type of plug-in. Note that most rendered plug-ins let you at least preview a section of a file in real time.

There are several different plug-in formats. One big difference is between rendered and real-time plug-ins. Rendered plug-ins apply an effect to digital audio, but not in real time; you have to wait for it to process, then listen to the results. Real-time plug-ins let you tweak parameters and hear the results immediately (although there may be a slight response lag with slower systems). If you like the results, you can then apply the processing to the file which changes it permanently.

Another differentiation is host-based (or native-based) vs. hardware-based. Hardware-based plug-ins run only with certain specialized hardware designed for digital signal processing. Host-based plug-ins use the computer's microprocessor to do any needed digital signal processing, and therefore require no specialized hardware.

Because host-based plug-ins place a load on the CPU, there are limits as to how many plug-ins you can use with a software program. This is mostly a concern with multitrack software where you might run lots of plug-ins; with mastering applications, it's unlikely most modern computers will run out of processing power.

Make sure any plug-ins you purchase are compatible with formats supported by your digital audio editor. Here are the most common formats.

❖ DirectX (Windows). This standard, originated by Microsoft, is very common.

❖ VST (Windows, Mac). Steinberg's cross-platform standard for plug-ins is very popular, and has been embraced by most plug-in manufacturers.

❖ MAS (Mac). The MOTU Audio System plug-ins are compatible with Mark of the Unicorn's Digital Performer software.

❖ TDM (Mac). Originated by Digidesign, Time Domain Multiplexing plug-ins were designed specifically to run with Digidesign's Pro Tools hardware. Non-Digidesign software may support these plug-ins if you are using Digidesign hardware.

❖ AudioSuite (Mac). Also from Digidesign, AudioSuite plug-ins are rendered effects.

❖ RTAS (Mac). Another Digidesign format, Real Time AudioSuite plug-ins are like AudioSuite plug-ins, but run in real time.

For most digital audio editing software, you will likely use DirectX or VST for Windows, and VST for the Mac.

Many programs have a "CPU meter" that shows how much power is being used. Compare its readings before and after loading a plug-in to see how much power a plug-in requires.

VST plug-ins are usually made in both Windows and Mac versions. Mac VST plug-ins cannot be used directly in Windows systems, and vice-versa.

Plug-ins compatible with the VST 2.0 and DirectX 8 specifications have the potential for parameter automation where you can store a series of control moves for later playback (e.g., change EQ over the course of a song).

Note that there are workarounds to "incompatible" plug-in formats. Example: FXpansion's VST-DX Adapter puts a "wrapper" around VST effects that makes them look like DirectX effects to DirectX-only software.

Inserting Plug-ins

Each program has its own way of inserting plug-ins.

Steinberg's WaveLab has a master section with six series "slots" for plug-ins. Clicking next to a slot calls up a list of available plug-ins. Groups of plug-ins can also be categorized to make finding them easier.

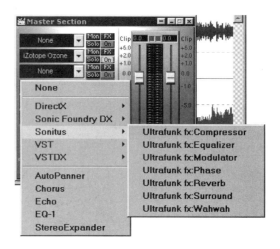

One of the cleverest options is an effects matrix (as used by TC Works' Spark and BIAS VBox, both of which accept VST-compatible effects). Effects can connect in series (where an effect output feeds a subsequent effect input) or in parallel where an effect output can feed several effect inputs whose outputs are then mixed together. Furthermore, the Spark FX Machine matrix and BIAS VBox matrix can also function as plug-ins in some non-VST systems, allowing you to use VST plug-ins with theoretically incompatible systems like MOTU's Digital Performer.

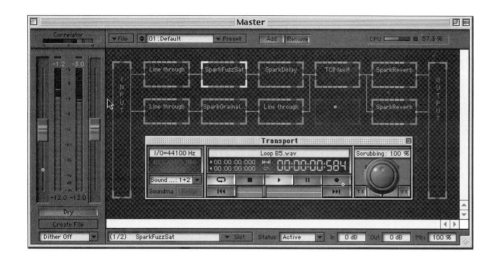

TC Works' Spark offers a matrix of slots into which you can insert effects.

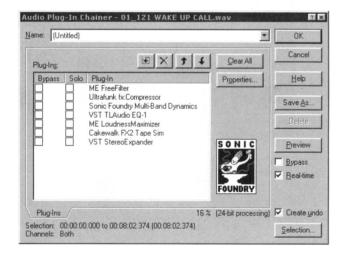

Sonic Foundry's Sound Forge has a plug-in chaining function where you can place plug-ins in series.

Parametric EQ

Equalization helps achieve a balanced response over the audible frequency spectrum.

Parametric EQ Basics

A parametric equalizer (EQ) is an exceptionally versatile way to adjust frequency response. It typically includes 4 to 8 audio filtering bands. Each band can boost (make more prominent) or cut (make less prominent) a specific part of the frequency spectrum.

A typical 4-band parametric EQ (from Cakewalk). Note the three controls along the right side. The four buttons select a band for editing.

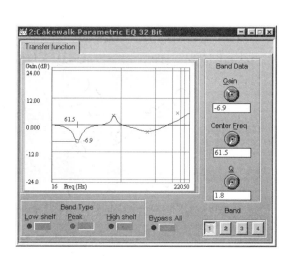

Parametric Controls

Each parametric band has at least three controls.

Frequency determines where the boosting or cutting takes place. Example: if the high frequencies need boosting, you would dial in a high frequency.

Boost/cut changes the response. Boosting increases the level in the chosen frequency range. Cutting decreases the level.

The amount of boost or cut is specified in *decibels* (dB). A change of 6dB doubles the level (−6dB halves it) which is a considerable amount. Changes of no more than 1 or 2dB are common in mastering. Even changes of a few tenths of a dB can make a difference.

A *decibel* is an audio unit of measurement that represents the smallest change in level the untrained ear can discern.

Bandwidth (also called Resonance or Q) sets the range of frequencies affected by the boost or cut, from broad to narrow. Broader settings are gentler, and used for general tone shaping. Narrow settings generally help solve specific response problems. Example: Suppose there is some 60Hz hum on a recording. Setting a very narrow cut at 60Hz will get rid of the hum, without affecting other frequencies.

Variations

Some parametric EQs have an additional parameter for changing the response (the manner in which the filter boosts or cuts).

CD Tracks 1 to 9 have examples of music passed through various equalization curves, such as bandpass, lowpass, high shelf, etc.

The most common parametric EQ response, bandpass, boosts or cuts a band of frequencies.

Bandpass boost at 1kHz. The bandwidth is 1 octave wide.

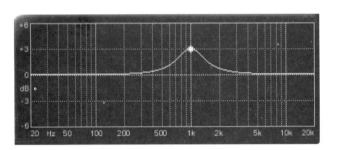

Bandpass filter cutting response at 1kHz.

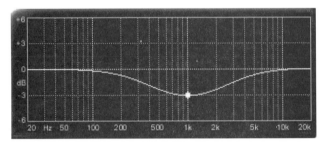

However, there are other possible response options.

Lowpass (also called high cut) progressively reduces response above a certain frequency. The reduction in response is greater toward the spectrum's higher frequencies. A typical application is removing hiss.

Lowpass response is down −3dB at 2kHz; high frequency response diminishes progressively from there.

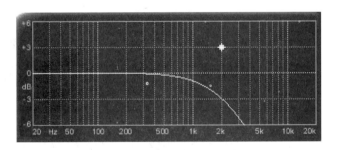

Highpass (also called low cut) progressively reduces response below a certain frequency. The lower the frequency, the greater the reduction. This is sometimes used to remove subsonic (very low frequency) energy.

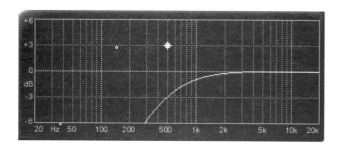

Highpass response is down −3dB at 500Hz; low frequency response diminishes progressively from there.

Notch is an ultra-steep bandpass that takes out one specific frequency. Example: Notching can remove a monitor's vertical oscillator frequency (a 15kHz signal that may bleed into mics when recording near a computer).

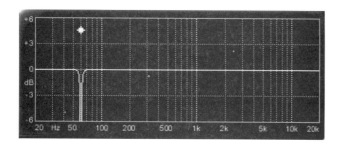

A very steep notch at 60Hz can help get rid of hum. For Europe, choose 50Hz.

A shelving response starts boosting or cutting at the selected frequency, but this boost or cut extends outward the extremes of the audio spectrum. Shelving stages have controls for frequency and boost/cut. There is no bandwidth control.

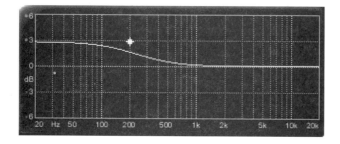

This low shelf boosts low frequencies by 3dB. Upon reaching 3dB of boost, the response hits a "shelf" and doesn't boost any more.

This high shelf boosts high frequencies by 3dB, and again the response hits a shelf past a certain point.

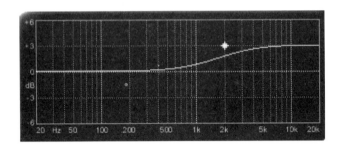

Some parametric EQs dedicate different stages to different response curves; with other types, any stage can have any response.

This typical parametric plug-in (by D Sound) offers seven stages. Each stage can have any of the responses mentioned above. Here's what each number means.

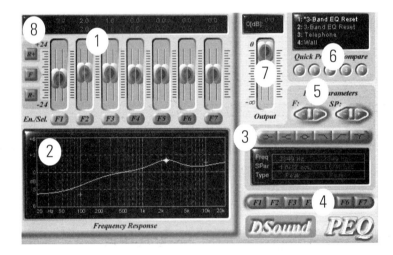

1 These sliders provide the boost/cut function for each stage.

2 The graph shows the frequency response that results from the current parameter values. You can drag points on the graph to change response which may be faster than entering a frequency and using the sliders to set the boost or cut amount.

3 This is the filter response selection strip.

4 Here is where you choose the stage to be edited if you want to do numeric parameter editing (**5**).

5 These controls set frequency and bandwidth for the stage selected in (**4**).

6 The preset area lets you save specific control settings for future recall.

7 The output control can trim the volume if there's enough boosting to cause overload, or increase the output if you've done a lot of cutting.

8 The readout above each slider displays the amount of boost or cut. With this particular plug-in, the right and left channels can have different frequency, boost/cut, and bandwidth settings.

Applying Parametric EQ

Your first step in mastering should be to aim for a balanced response through equalization.

Choosing the Right Filter Response

You'll use the bandpass response most with parametric stages. As different instruments occupy different parts of the frequency spectrum, you can almost remix a song by applying EQ properly. Example: If the bass isn't loud enough, boost the low frequencies. Or, increase vocal intelligibility by boosting the upper midrange.

CD Tracks 10 and 11 are excerpts of songs before and after adding equalization.

A highpass filter may be useful if there is subsonic energy in a tune; set it to pass only frequencies above 20Hz.

> Subsonic energy can't be heard, but uses up dynamic range and should be eliminated if possible.

Shelving filter responses are good for a general lift in the bass and/or treble regions. They can also tame bass and/or treble regions that are too prominent.

The notch response can be useful if some instrument has a resonant frequency that sticks out, and a bandpass setting would be too broad.

Equalization Tips

❖ Equalization is very powerful—use it sparingly. When you make a change that sounds right, cut it in half. In other words, if boosting a signal by 2dB at 4kHz seems to improve the tune's sound, pull back the boost to 1dB and live with the sound for a while. It's easy to get stuck in a spiral where if you boost the treble, the bass then lacks prominence. So you boost the bass, but now the midrange seems weak, so you boost that, and now you're back to where you started.

Oddly enough, some digital filter algorithms may cause distortion if you *cut* levels. After doing an operation, always listen to a processed file, and check that the waveform isn't clipping. If there's a problem, you can always undo the operation.

❖ Excessive boosting can cause distortion. If necessary, trim the EQ's output control to tame the overall level. Better yet, remix the song—the need for excessive boosting usually means there's a problem with the mix.

❖ The ear is most sensitive in the midrange and upper midrange. Be wary of harshness when boosting in this region.

❖ Compare the overall response of your CD with commercially-available, well-recorded and mastered CDs.
This is a great "reality check." Compare CDs at the
same approximate level, or the comparison won't be as
valid.

This technique is so valuable that there are programs
that can compare the frequency response curves of two
different recordings, as well as superimpose the frequency spectrum characteristics of one tune on to
another—which is the subject of the next chapter.

Curve Analysis/ Matching

4

Wouldn't it be great if your tune's overall equalization could match a well-mastered hit song? The main tool for doing this is your ears. Compare your work with something that sounds great, and come as close as you can: If your recording sounds muddy compared to the reference, trim back the bass; if your guitars don't stand out, bring up the midrange to compensate. But the right software can also help.

Spectrum Analyzers

Most digital audio editing programs include some type of spectrum analysis function.

A spectrum analyzer divides the spectrum into multiple frequency bands, and shows the distribution of energy in each band. The Y-axis represents level in decibels, the X-axis shows frequency in Hertz.

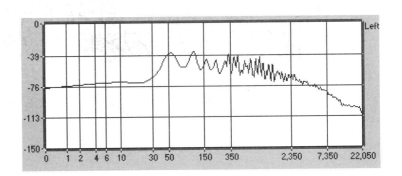

The dance mix shown in Sound Forge's Spectrum Analysis tool above has most of its energy in the range of 50 to 2,300Hz. The 50Hz peak corresponds to the kick drum. Above 2,300Hz, response drops off. This avoids a "screechy," overly-bright high end.

At the low end, response drops off dramatically below 50Hz. In fact, an octave lower (25Hz), the response is down by about −35dB.

Analyzing commercially-available recordings can teach you a lot. This graph shows a typical Fatboy Slim curve (light line) compared to Madonna's Ray of Light (dark line). Fatboy Slim's is much brighter, while Ray of Light has a prominent kick that shows up in the bass range.

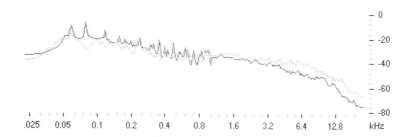

Spectrum Display Meets EQ

Some programs integrate the spectrum display with processing, rather than making it a stand-alone function.

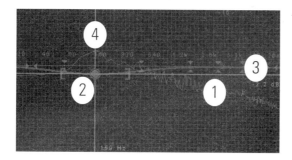

Above is the parametric EQ screen from iZotope's Ozone mastering software.

1 This line shows the overall distribution of energy.

2 The "crosshairs" is pulling down the EQ curve (**3**) around 150Hz where there's a massive bump (**4**). This results in a less bass-heavy sound.

A graphic equalizer splits the spectrum into a large number of bands, each of which has a boost/cut control. Unlike a parametric equalizer, frequency and bandwidth are fixed, not variable.

Steinberg's Freefilter is an extremely versatile spectrum analyzer/filter. Instead of being based on a parametric equalizer, it uses a *graphic equalizer* approach.

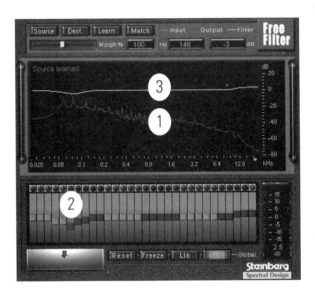

You'll note a button marked Log and another called Lin; Log is selected. This changes how the spectrum is displayed. Logarithmic mode best approximates how the ear responds to music, and is preferred over Linear.

1 Shows the tune's spectral response. It follows the same curve as most pop music, with a relatively strong bass and midrange, and highs that taper off.

2 The row of controls are boost/cut controls for the 30 adjustable frequency bands. They are set to pull down the bass a bit, and add a slight lift at high frequencies.

3 This line shows the frequency response change that results from the boost/cut control settings.

An even more interesting Freefilter feature is that it can "learn" one tune's spectral response and apply it to another tune. A "morph" slider determines how closely your tune adopts the reference's curve, from a very slight influence to an exact match.

Arboretum's Ionizer program can also apply one song's spectral response to another.

While useful, there are limitations. If the reference tune has a strong kick drum and weak bass, the curve will show a strong bass bump because of the kick. If you apply that to a tune with a moderate kick and strong bass, the bass will likely be boosted too high.

On the CD examples of applying curves, the mixed, unmastered song has a broad range of frequencies, all fairly prominent in the mix. Applying the Ray of Light curve doesn't make a huge difference, because the two tunes have a similar response. However, it does bring out the kick, and lays the guitars further back.

CD Tracks 12 to 15 have examples that use Freefilter to impress one song's response curve on another.

The Fatboy Slim curve is super-bright, whereas the Spice Girls curve has the high and midrange peaks characteristic of "pop" mixes.

Morphs on these curves are around 50%, as 100% morphing is usually too much. For example, morphing the Fatboy Slim curve at 100% produces an almost unbearable treble boost, but 50% give a pleasing treble "lift."

The bottom line: This kind of software isn't magic, but it can be very educational and sometimes, just what's needed.

About Dynamics 5

Along with EQ, dynamics control is a crucial element of mastering.

Dynamic range is the difference between a recording's loudest and softest sections. Live music has an extremely wide dynamic range; prior to the CD, it was impossible to capture this range on vinyl or tape. Setting levels high to record soft passages led to overloading on peaks, while setting levels low enough to prevent peaks from distorting obscured soft passages with noise.

Limiters and *compressors* used to be different types of devices. Modern dynamics control plug-ins can provide either and/or both processes.

Initially engineers adjusted the gain manually while recording—turning down on peaks, turning up during quiet parts—to restrict dynamic range. But it's hard to do this fast and consistently, so devices called *compressors* and *limiters* were invented to restrict dynamic range automatically.

Although CDs have a very wide dynamic range, your listening environment may not due to background noise from air conditioning, road noise in cars, etc. Using compression can help lift music above the noise.

Now you know why TV commercials seem much louder than the shows: they're highly compressed.

How much compression to use is controversial. Many listeners think "louder is better," so pop music records are compressed—sometimes to the point of destroying dynamic range—to sound "hotter." DJs prefer highly-compressed dance music to minimize level variations, thus giving them more control over level via the DJ mixer's faders. Classical and jazz recordings use little compression.

About Headroom

Any system will have a maximum acceptable signal level. Going any higher results in distortion. Most engineers try to keep peaks a few dB below maximum, to leave a little headroom in case of unexpected loud parts.

CD Track 16 shows what happens when a digital system distorts. It's not pretty.

About Normalization

A signal should also not peak too low below the available headroom, as that throws away level. The normalization process calculates the difference between a recording's highest peak and the maximum available level, then increases the recording's overall level so that its highest peak reaches the maximum level.

Normalization doesn't always have to be to the maximum level. You could normalize a signal to, for example, −3dB below maximum.

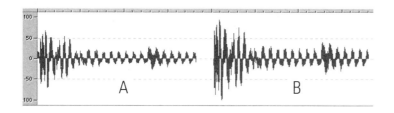

Waveforms A and B are identical, except B has been normalized so its peaks attain the maximum available level.

You might think this makes it easy to match song levels—just normalize them. This is true only if they have the same average, not just peak, level. A song where everyone's playing as loud as they can has a high peak and average level. A sparse ballad will usually have a lower average level, even if some peaks are relatively high. So, you may need to reduce the super-loud song's level a bit so it doesn't overpower the ballad.

What works for me: I normalize all my tunes, but assemble them in a CD-burning program that allows changing each tune's level. As I listen to the tracks playing together, I lower the level of tunes that seem overly loud.

Why Compression Makes Songs Louder

Compression reduces the level of peaks that are above a certain threshold. Here's how this process can make recordings sound louder.

1 The peak hits 0dB, so the sound can't be made louder without causing distortion:

2 Compression has lowered the peak (highlighted):

3 Now we can raise the gain so that the peak goes up to 0, bringing the rest of the signal up along with it. You can see this signal has more overall amplitude than the original one:

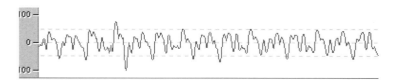

Use Your Judgement

Compression is not always a transparent process. Over-compressing gives a pinched, unpleasant sound with "pumping" and "breathing." The overcompressed example on the CD is louder, but the sound quality is terrible.

CD Track 17 demonstrates normal vs. overcompressed sounds.

One of the more difficult decisions for beginning mastering engineers is how much to compress. Bands will often clamor for the loudest recording possible, but resist the temptation. I do a lot of mastering for dance music; while I try to make it as loud as possible, I back off if the compression sounds obvious.

Remember the idea of comparing your recording to other commercially-available ones? Just remember that some hit records are poorly mastered by even the most relaxed standards. Seek out albums mastered by acknowledged experts like Bob Ludwig, Doug Sax, Bernie Grundman, Randy Kling, and others to get an idea of what good mastering really is—and compare your recordings to theirs.

Compression

Compression is often mis-applied because we can hear very fine pitch changes, but not ampli-tude. So, there is a ten-dency to overcompress until you can "hear the effect," which gives an unnatural sound. Until you've trained your ears to recognize subtle amounts of compression, keep an eye on the gain reduction meters (described later) to avoid overcompressing.

Compressor Parameters

Compressors all have the same general controls. Here's a typical plug-in compressor (Ultrafunk fx:compressor).

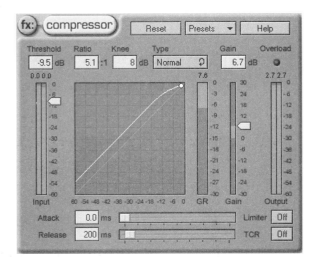

Threshold sets the level at which compression begins, in this case, −9.5dB. Above this level, the output increases at a lesser rate than a corresponding input change. With lower thresholds, more of the signal gets compressed, and the peaks become lower.

Ratio defines how much the output signal changes for a given input signal change. Examples: With 2:1 compression, a 2dB increase at the input yields a 1dB increase at the output. With 4:1 compression, a 16dB increase at the input gives a 4dB increase at the output. Higher ratios increase the effect of the compression, and tend to sound more unnatural. With an "infinite" compression ratio, the output will refuse to go past a certain point, no matter how much you pump up the input.

Attack determines how long it takes for the compression to start once it senses an input level change. Longer attack times let more of a signal's natural dynamics through, but remember, those signals are not being compressed. With analog recording, the tape would absorb any overload caused by sudden transients. With digital, those transients distort as soon as they exceed 0dB.

Gain compensates for the volume drop that occurs from squashing peaks. Turn this control up until the compressed signal's peak levels reach 0dB.

Release sets the time required for the compressor to stop affecting the signal once the input passes below the threshold. Longer settings work well with program material, as the level changes are more gradual and produce a less noticeable effect.

Knee controls how rapidly the compression kicks in. With soft knee, when the input exceeds the threshold, the compression ratio is less at first, then increases up to the specified ratio as the input increases. With hard knee response, as soon as the input signal crosses the threshold, it's subject to the full amount of compression. Use "hard" to clamp levels down tight, and "soft" for gentler compression effects.

The large graph shows the actual input/output curve. Note how the output level increases at a slower rate for higher input levels. That's what compression is all about.

CD track 18 has a drum loop with a 0ms attack, and one with a 20ms attack. The second one has a sharper, stronger attack, but a slightly lower overall level.
(Drum loop courtesy Discrete Drums, www.discretedrums.com)

CD track 19 shows how a short release setting affects drums. This produces an effect where hitting the cymbal modulates the entire kit with a pumping kind of sound.
(Drum loop courtesy Discrete Drums, www.discretedrums.com)

Miscellaneous Parameters

A *limiter* is like a governor on a motor: signals will not exceed the threshold, although excessive limiting will result in distortion.

Most compressors have parameters in addition to the standard ones described above. This one has a Type control that chooses between a normal or "vintage" response, a *Limiter* switch that clamps the output to odB, and a Transient Controlled Release (TCR) switch that automatically optimizes the release time for different program material.

Others compressors can increase the output control automatically to compensate for the decreased level from lowering peaks, or choose whether the compression responds to peak or average signal levels. (Choose peak if the material is very percussive, or average for standard program material.)

How to Adjust Compression

Compression is difficult to set up correctly. Here are some tips:

❖ The gain reduction meter shows how much the input signal's level is being reduced at any given moment. You generally don't want more than 6dB of reduction, and even that's stretching it. To reduce the amount of gain reduction, either raise the threshold, or reduce the compression ratio.

❖ Adjust the gain control so that the output meter indicator comes as close to odB as possible, but never hits or exceeds it.

❖ The most important controls are threshold and ratio. To really clamp down on peaks, choose a high ratio (10:1 or greater) and a relatively high threshold (around −1 to −6dB).

Lower thresholds won't just tame the occasional peak, but also reduce the overall signal.

❖ For a more natural sound, use lower compression ratios (1.5:1 to 3:1).

❖ With no attack time, peaks are clamped instantly, producing the most drastic compression action. If it's crucial that the signal never hits 0 yet you want really high average levels, use zero attack time. It's probably better to use an attack time of 5 to 20ms to let through some peaks, even if it means a somewhat lower average signal level.

Attack times under 5ms may lead to clipping with high signal levels. But often, the clipping is short enough that it's not noticeable.

❖ Decay is not as critical as attack. Start in the 100 to 250ms range. Shorter times sound "livelier," longer times sound "smoother." But too short a time can give a choppy effect, while too long a release time homogenizes the sound.

❖ Use hard knee settings when controlling peaks is a priority. Use soft knee curves for a less colored sound.

❖ Some compressors include a function that automatically adjusts attack and decay times according to the signal passing through the system. This is often the best choice if you're new to compression.

Multiband Compression

7

If a standard compressor turns down the level due to a peak in the bass range, it's turning down the level for all frequencies, not just the bass. So, even if there aren't high frequency peaks, the highs will be reduced anyway.

A multiband compressor has several individual compression stages (typically four or five), each of which covers a particular frequency range. So, compression that occurs in one band doesn't affect the others.

Often, a solo function lets you audition an individual band so you can adjust it without being distracted by what's going on in the other bands.

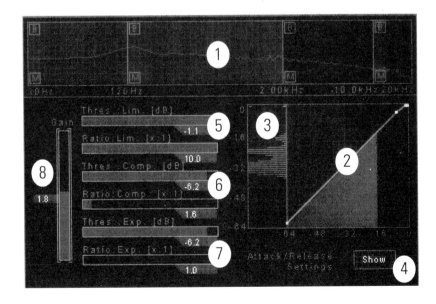

The depicted multiband compressor is a module in iZotope's Ozone mastering processor. Here's the story on the various functions:

1 This strip shows the four adjustable frequency bands. When you click on a band, the controls relate to that band only. Moving the bar between bands changes a band's frequency range.

2 This graph displays the compression curve.

3 The level histogram tracks level changes over time to show which levels occur most often.

4 To see the attack and release settings, you need to click on a button that brings up a separate page.

5 This plug-in has dedicated limiter parameters. With the settings shown, any peaks above −1.1dB are clamped to that level.

6 These are the traditional compression threshold/ratio controls. The threshold for this band is set at −6.2dB, and the compression ratio at 1.6:1—a fairly light setting. Although there is no "knee" parameter, being able to adjust limiting and compression separately can produce curves with different levels of "hardness."

7 There are also dedicated parameters for expansion. Expansion is the opposite of compression: Below a certain threshold, the output level decreases at a faster rate than the input level. Expansion can push low-level noise in the background by setting the expansion threshold just above the noise level, then setting a fairly high ratio.

An infinitely high expansion ratio causes the expander to act like a noise gate, effectively removing any signals below the threshold.

Level Maximizers

8

Level Maximizer Basics

CD Track 20 plays a reference file, and Track 21 processes it with the Waves L1, set for about 6dB of extra level.

With the trend toward ever-louder CDs, new and more potent strains of dynamics control have appeared called level maximizers. These restrict dynamic range by essentially re-drawing peaks to go no higher than a settable threshold. It's then possible to increase the overall file's level by whatever amount the peaks were reduced. For a given perceived level increase, this can produce less obvious effects than traditional limiting or compression.

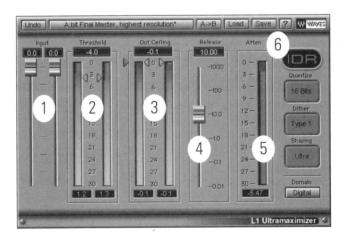

The Waves L1, shown above, was the first plug-in to maximize levels without standard compression techniques. Controls for this type of plug-in are quite simple.

1 The Input level controls trim the input signal, if needed.

2 Threshold sets the point above which peaks are re-drawn. Pulling the triangles downwards lowers the threshold. Lowering the threshold by −3dB effectively raises the overall level by 3dB.

3 Out Ceiling sets an absolute output limit; no signal will exceed the indicated output.

4 Release works similarly to standard compressors—it sets the time for the system to recover after being hit by a peak.

5 The Gain Reduction meter shows the amount of attenuation being applied to a signal at any moment.

6 The IDR function has more to do with improving the output resolution, using various dithering processes (see next chapter).

Using Level Maximizers

Because it's possible to really push these and not hear too many audible artifacts, it's tempting to just keep pumping up the volume. But if you're working with a reasonably well-mixed tune, boosting it by 3dB or so will be plenty. Unrelenting loudness and lack of dynamics ultimately leads to listener fatigue.

Dithering

9

Most digital audio editors process 16-bit files using higher resolution, like 24, 32, or even 64 bits, because processing two 16-bit signals can produce results that exceed 16 bits of resolution.

However, CDs accommodate only 16-bit audio. Truncation (simply removing 8 bits from the higher-resolution signal) can cause distortion at low levels. Dithering adds controlled, low-level noise that smooths out this distortion, and improves low-level sound quality.

To minimize the noise's audibility, a noise-shaping process weights the noise spectrum toward bands outside the ear's peak response.

Always keep an undithered copy of your unmastered audio. If you need to make changes later, work on the original and re-dither rather than work with dithered audio.

Dithering should be done only once during the course of a project, as the very last step in creating a 16-bit stereo master file. Turn on (or plug in) dithering as you master your file; set it for the target number of bits (e.g., "16" for CD), and choose the dithering and noise-shaping algorithms that sound best. When you apply the dithering (if needed) and save the file, it will have the dither characteristics you specified.

Different dithering algorithms sound different. Deciding on whose brand of dither you like best is not unlike wine-tasting.

Specialized Tools 10

As mastering becomes accessible to a wider group of people, the demand for more specialized plug-ins grows. Here just some of the new tools designed to help mastering engineers.

Vintage Device Emulators

There are certain "classic" pieces of hardware which are being analyzed and re-born as plug-ins. Sometimes the plug-in tries to duplicate the original as closely as possible, like Steinberg's TLAudio-1 EQ. Others take a more general approach, and aim for a vintage "vibe" rather than a specific piece of gear.

Steinberg's Quadrafuzz emulates a multi-band distortion processor I designed in the 80s, but improves upon the original in many ways, such as adding programmability. While the concept of deliberately introducing distortion while mastering may seem bizarre, it can give an "edge" without affecting dynamics as much as compression. Some engineers consider light distortion as their "secret weapon" for mastering.

CD Track 22 processes Track 20 with Steinberg's Quadrafuzz.

The PSP Vintage Warmer combines old-school compression, overdrive, and high/low frequency equalization. It's not as sonically neutral as something like the Waves L1, preferring instead to give the option to "hype" the sound if desired.

CD Track 23 processes Track 20 through the PSP Vintage Warmer.

There are also devices that simulate the distortion produced by analog tape. While this might seem like a step backward, these processors offer many opportunities to the adventurous.

CD Track 24 processes Track 20 through the Cakewalk FX2 Tape Sim.

Bass Enhancers

In addition to EQ, there are other ways to enhance bass. The Waves MaxxBass adds harmonics to the bass, so it can stand out better in systems that lack good bass response. Other plug-ins do the opposite, adding sub-harmonics to give the bass more depth. Yet another approach is to add a stage of compression, optimized for low frequencies, to bring out the bass.

Stereo Image Enhancers

These create "super-stereo" effects that widen the stereo image, particularly in the high frequency range where the ear is most sensitive to directionality. Some of these devices use phase changes to enhance the stereo image, and therefore may give unpredictable results if played back in mono. Always check the response in mono when using any plug-in or device that alters stereo separation.

Harmonic Enhancers

This type of plug-in adds a high-frequency "sheen" without the use of EQ. As with bass enhancement, there are many ways to do this. One approach is to add a very slight amount of distortion, use a steep highpass filter to remove everything but the highest harmonics of the distortion, then mix this signal back in with the main signal. If used sparingly, the minute amounts of high-frequency distortion can give increased clarity and stereo separation, without the "tinniness" you might encounter with standard EQ.

Reverb

Reverb is not used a lot in mastering, but there are circumstances where it can help. One application is to cover up a cut or splice in the song if this problem was not addressed during mixdown. Another is with material that was primarily recorded direct (i.e., instruments plugged directly into the console), as reverberation can add a little space.

> CD Track 25 has a before-and-after-mastering example of audio captured during a seminar on Mac vs. PC. Note how the reverb adds a little more depth.

Troubleshooting

11

Digital audio editors don't need as powerful a computer as something like a multitrack hard disk recorder, but plug-ins do place a load on the CPU.

You hear stuttering or crackles in the audio.

Unplug any plug-ins from the program. If that solves the problem, you need a faster processor, more memory, or both. Or, use fewer (or less CPU-intensive) plug-ins. Your program's "CPU meter" should indicate how much power is being used by the plug-ins. Another strong possibility is that your sound card driver needs updating.

Your program doesn't "see" a plug-in you've installed.

First, try re-booting the computer. If the problem persists, check your program's manual to see if there's a particular location or folder where the software expects to see plug-ins. Move the plug-in to the appropriate folder if needed, then re-boot.

You don't hear any audio.

Check any Preferences or Options menus in the program to make sure audio is being routed correctly from the program to an appropriate audio output. Also check the obvious—is the mixer master level control turned up?

Operation is highly unstable.

Use only legal versions of programs. "Cracked" versions often cause serious problems.

FAQ

My tunes sound great at home, but terrible over other systems. Why?

This indicates a monitoring or acoustics problem. Because you are playing back from the system you mastered on, if there's a problem in your setup, you won't notice it until you play your music over a more accurate system. Use near-field monitors, and if possible, treat your room acoustically to minimize reflections and standing waves.

Good speakers are really expensive, but I can pick up a nice set of headphones for much less. Is it practical to master using headphones?

Headphones are a good "reality check" for hearing small problems you might not notice otherwise. However, they give a hyper-detailed sound that is not representative of typical listening conditions.

Why do my CDs sound much softer than commercially-available CDs?

Consider using a level maximizer or multiband compressor plug-in to further restrict the dynamic range, then raise the signal's overall level. But if your music sounds good and isn't abnormally low, don't worry. Many current releases are way "over-maximized" to produce the loudest possible sound, at the expense of a pleasing dynamic range.

Is it important to normalize a CD's cuts to a value lower than 0, like −0.01dB or so?

If a tune has peaks that hit 0 for more than a few milliseconds, it may be rejected by a CD pressing plant on the assumption that those peaks represent distortion. Use a program's level scan function (usually part of the normalization process) to check the tune's maximum level. If it's 0, normalize the file to −0.01dB. You can also use this technique with tunes that do have distortion (hey, accidents happen!) to make it look like the CD isn't distorted.

Should I pre-master a song before handing it over to a professional mastering engineer?

Never! Give the engineer the raw, unprocessed mix. Don't even add fades; add them while mastering.

How much does each step of the mastering process change the sound?

CD Tracks 26 to 30 go through each step of a typical mastering process.

Each step by itself may not make much of a difference, but add them all together, and you'll hear a significant change. CD Tracks 26 to 30 take a song from raw mix to a mastered part of a movie soundtrack. It also shows how plug-ins can make a relatively loud tune with a consistent level which was a requirement for this movie.

By the way, Track 31 is a song of mine that I mastered recently. It's included as a "real-world" example of recording, mixing, and mastering in the home studio.